# Notes to My Children

on getting, being, and staying married

Jo Lief

**Andrews McMeel
Publishing**

Kansas City

D0503437

www.andrewsmcmeel.com

99 00 01 02 03 TWP 10 9 8 7 6 5 4 3 2 1

Library of Congress Cataloging-in-Publication Data

Lief, Jo.
    Notes to my children on getting, being, and staying married.
       p.    cm.
    ISBN 0-7407-0038-3 (hardcover)
    1. Marriage.
HQ734.L55    1999
306.81—dc21                                          98-45947
                                                     CIP

ATTENTION: SCHOOLS AND BUSINESSES

Andrews McMeel books are available at quantity discounts with bulk purchase for educational, business, or sales promotional use. For information, please write to: Special Sales Department, Andrews McMeel Publishing, 4520 Main Street, Kansas City, Missouri 64111.

To: _____
From: _____
Notes: _____
_____
_____
_____
_____

To my husband, Todd

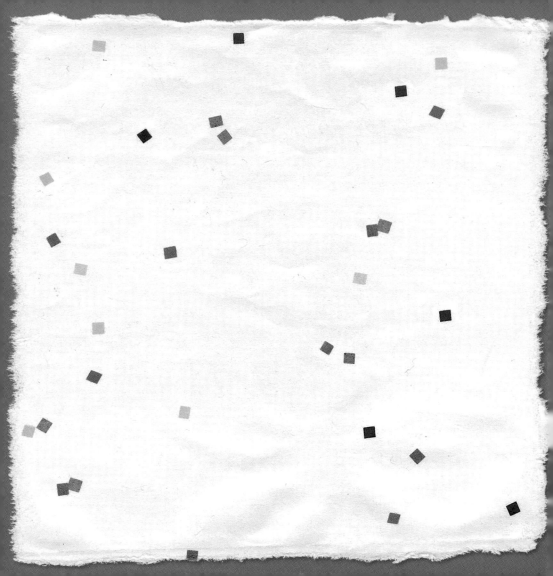

# *Acknowledgments*

## Thanks!

To Amy and Jason, who became engaged and inspired me to "speak" to them in this way.

To Amy, who surprised and delighted me by submitting *Notes to My Children* to her agent.

To Jeremy, for connecting me with Andrews McMeel.

To Stephanie, my editor, who patiently guided me through the prepublication process.

To all the enthusiastic readers, including Michel, Amy, Jason, Todd, Linda, Ann, and Paul, as well as other friends and my Tuesday morning group, who loved this book and spurred me on!

And to Linda Eisenberg, my art teacher, who encouraged me and helped me create the art.

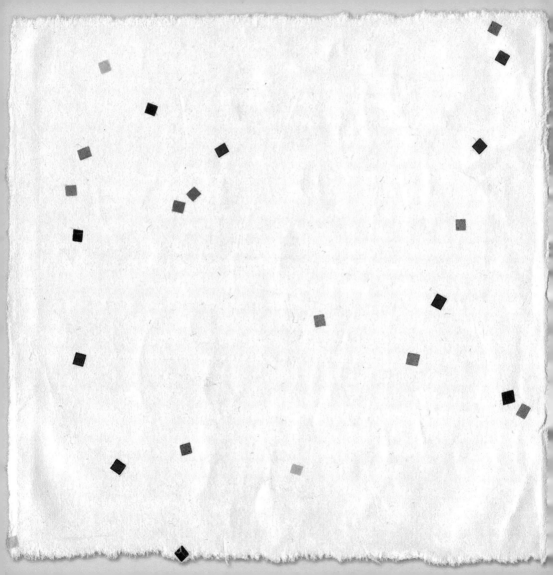

# Notes to My Children

on getting, being, and staying married

Believe in the institution.

Two ARE better than one.

Commitment is the ground.
It's staying power even when your relationship
is on a roller-coaster ride.

Delight in your differences.

Relish your similarities.

Men and women
ARE
different!

Be accepting of each other's limitations.

One person can't fill all your needs.

Take turns.

Take risks.

Surprise each other.

Ask for what you want.

Be grateful when you get it.

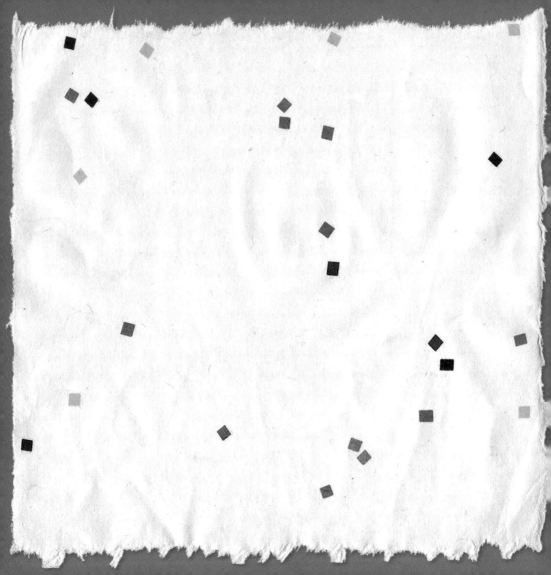

Give
generously
of your love.

Play together and laugh a lot.
When you notice
        you've stopped playing,

STOP.

Focus on playing again.

*Give each other space.*

*Sometimes togetherness is too hard.*

*Those are the times to take a nap or a walk.*

Don't say yes when you mean no.

It's okay to be "selfish" sometimes.

Don't let obligations fill your life.

Fighting is normal.

*Talking out your feelings brings closeness.*

Pamper your partner if he/she is sick or blue.

Vacation often.

(Rest restores and contrast balances.)

Separate getaways are okay, too.

Make your home your favorite place to be.

Move if it isn't.

Collect treasures.

Reminisce.

Anticipate.

Love means something different to everyone.

Just make sure you like each other.

Just because you're married doesn't mean you
should stop going out on dates.
Take turns planning dates for each other.

*Have common interests and friends.*

Have separate interests and friends.

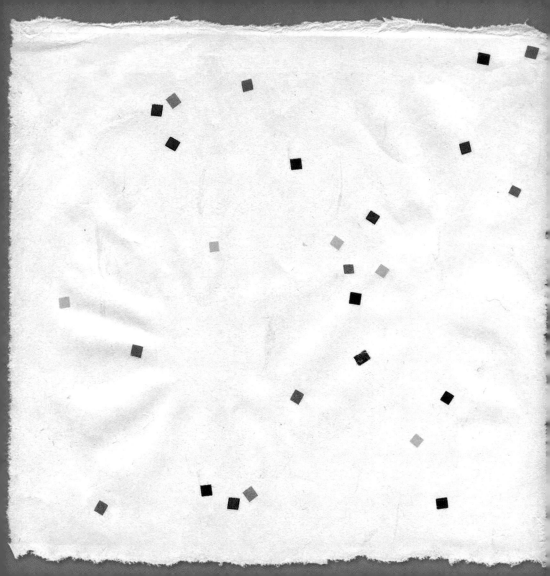

Make birthdays a big deal!

Tell her she's beautiful.

Tell him he's handsome.

Feeling sexy comes and goes.
Cuddling is always good.

Relax. Take a hot bath.

Take a hot bath together.

Wash each other's hair.

Men are visual.

They love to see women
looking beautiful.

Women are auditory.

They love to hear whispers of
endearment.

Create shared rituals:
a Sunday walk to get the paper . . .
a weekly ethnic dinner . . .
TV shows you both love . . .
et cetera.

Learn something new together.

Tell your partner your dreams.

Dreams are for coming true.

*Take lots of photographs.*

Do you like poetry? Try it.
Read to each other.

Dance and listen to music.
Get to know each other's favorites.
Sing even if you can't carry a tune.

Remember, there once was a time before TV.

Culinary skill is a virtue.

It's erotic in a man

and nurturing in a woman.

Cook for each other.

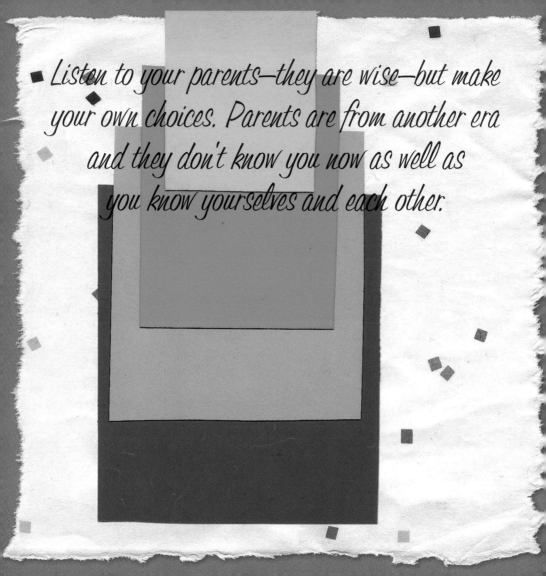

Listen to your parents—they are wise—but make your own choices. Parents are from another era and they don't know you now as well as you know yourselves and each other.

Listen slowly and carefully to hear
where the other person's coming from.
This will get you everywhere.
Being defensive will
get you nowhere.

Encourage curiosity.

Experiment.

Count your blessings—regularly.

Goodwill helps a lot.

Always remember the thrill of your first days and months together, but let them be the foundation —not the requirement—of your love.

Read this book again in two years.